BALL SPORTS

Barbara C. Bourassa

Written by Barbara C. Bourassa
Edited, designed and picture researched by
  Starry Dog Books Ltd
Consultant Steven Downes, of the Sports Journalists'
  Association www.sportsjournalists.co.uk

Publisher Steve Evans
Creative Director Zeta Davies
Senior Editor Hannah Ray

Printed and bound in China

Website information is correct at time of going to press. However, the publishers cannot accept liability for any information or links found on third-party websites.

All the sports in this book involve differing degrees of difficulty and the publisher would strongly advise that none of the activities mentioned is undertaken without adult supervision or the guidance of a professional coach.

Words in **bold** can be found in the Glossary on pages 30–31.

CONTENTS

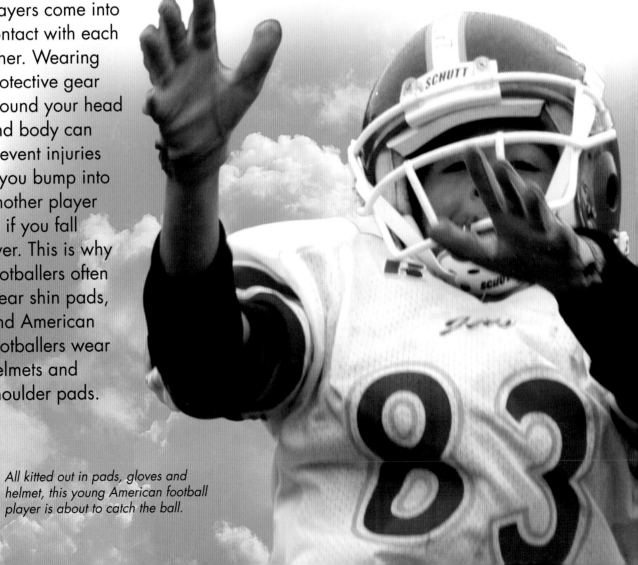

THE SUBJECT of ball sports is a large one: it includes any activity that is based around a ball, from batting a beach ball around on the sand to scoring a goal with a football. This book will focus on well-known, organized ball sports. Some of these, such as football and volleyball, are team sports; others, such as bowling, are more individual sports. All of them are fun and exciting to learn!

Getting kitted out

In many ball sports, players come into contact with each other. Wearing protective gear around your head and body can prevent injuries if you bump into another player or if you fall over. This is why footballers often wear shin pads, and American footballers wear helmets and shoulder pads.

▶ All kitted out in pads, gloves and helmet, this young American football player is about to catch the ball.

TAKE IT SLOWLY!

Before you run out of the door and start kicking, throwing or spiking your ball of choice, it is important to keep a few things in mind. Remember, the **amateur** or **professional** players that you may follow are very experienced at what they're doing. Some of them are international champions in their sport, and have been practising for years and years; others are still amateurs, but have trained with professional **coaches** for some time. So don't expect to perform at the same levels or complete the same moves that they do! First you need to learn the basics of your chosen sport.

Mastering the game

As any good coach will tell you, learning a new sport means understanding and mastering the basics. You'll need to look after your equipment carefully, and do lots of practice. All sports, from basketball to bowling, keep you healthy and active. Remember to drink plenty of water, eat well and take breaks whenever you need to – whether you are dribbling a basketball or getting ready to knock down bowling pins.

Keep safe

All sports involve a degree of danger, and some ball sports require more safety equipment than others. However, when they are played by the rules, they can all be fun and exciting to learn, so get ready for your new ball-sport adventure!

VOLLEYBALL can be played indoors on a court, or outside on the beach. Two teams stand separated by a high net. The aim of the **attacking** team is to hit the ball over the net and onto the ground on the other side. The **defending** team tries to hit the ball back over the net before it can touch the ground. If the players let the ball touch the ground, or fail to return it, the attacking team scores a point.

THE SCORING SYSTEM

The first team to score 25 points (and be two points ahead) wins the set. The team that wins the most sets out of five wins the match. The fifth set is usually played to 15 or 30 points, depending on the **league** or level of the players.

INDOOR VS. BEACH VOLLEYBALL

The rules and set-up of indoor and beach volleyball are slightly different. In beach volleyball, two or more players make up a team, and players can wear swimsuits and sunglasses. In indoor volleyball, six players make up a team. They wear numbered shirts and protective knee pads in case they fall on the hard court floor.

Serve, bump, spike

The game starts with the attacking team **serving** the ball over the net. To keep it from hitting the ground, one of the receiving team will **set**, **dig** or **bump** the ball, which means hitting it up into the air. His or her teammate can then attack by spiking the ball – jumping up high and hitting it sharply downwards back over the net.

◀ *Professional volleyball players often use an overhand serve, as seen here. If you are new to volleyball, an underhand serve is easier to learn.*

▶ *The player on the right in this game of beach volleyball has spiked the ball over the net. The player on the left has tried, unsuccessfully, to block it.*

JUNIOR VOLLEYBALL

Many beach volleyball competitions are designed just for junior players. These championship games are usually divided into three age categories: under 14, under 16 and under 18. Many of the best junior players are from the USA, Australia and Brazil.

Blocking the ball

The players receiving the spike try to block it, which means they **deflect** the ball before it hits the ground. Each team is allowed three hits to get the ball back over the net to the other team.

MOST young boys and girls love basketball. It's an easy game that needs only a basketball, a hoop attached to a post or high wall and lots of practice! Professionals, however, play on a large court with five players on each team, referees, uniforms and strict rules.

TALLEST?

According to the Guinness Book of World Records, the tallest professional basketball player is Gheorghe Muresan, who stands 2.31m tall. Gheorghe started playing for the Romanian national team at the age of 16.

Moving around the court

In the game of basketball, players try to move the ball to their end of the court. They can move it by dribbling (bouncing it up and down using their hands as they walk or run), passing (throwing or bouncing it to another player) or shooting (throwing it towards the basket). Simply carrying the ball, or 'travelling', is not allowed.

When one player tries to shoot a basket, players on the other team try to block the shot by lifting their arms.

Scoring points

Marked on the court around the basket is an arch (almost a semicircle). If you shoot the ball from inside the arch, either with a **jump shot** or from standing, and it goes in, you score two points. If you 'make a basket' from outside the arch, you score three points.

HOOP HEIGHT

In professional basketball, the rim of the basket is usually 3m from the ground. For children, the hoop height can vary according to age and ability. Some basketball hoops are designed so they can be raised or lowered.

▶ In a professional game of basketball, once a player gets the ball he or she must try to shoot a basket within 24 seconds. This is called the 24-second rule.

WOMEN'S OLYMPIC BASKETBALL

Men's basketball has been an Olympic sport since 1936, but women's basketball only became an Olympic sport in 1976. In recent years the women's medals have been dominated by the USA and teams from the former Soviet Union.

One-on-one

Playing basketball with just yourself and a friend is sometimes called 'one-on-one'. The name means just what it says: one player against one player. It is a fun and easy way to play basketball that allows you to practise shooting baskets and moving with the ball. You might also want to make up your own practice exercises. One easy exercise involves setting up a series of small cones and dribbling the ball between them.

Basketball is popular all over the world. These children are playing on a dirt court in the Kibera township in Nairobi, Kenya.

Shooting practice

In 'one-on-one', if you shoot a basket and score, the other player **gains possession** of the ball. Before he or she can shoot, the player must first dribble the ball outside the **key**, a rectangular area in front of the basket. If you shoot a basket and miss, either of you can try to catch the ball as it comes off the backboard (the large white area behind the basket). However, you cannot score without first moving or dribbling the ball outside the key.

BALL AND BASKET FACTS

A basketball hoop is closely related in size and shape to a basketball. Professional male basketball players play with a ball that measures about 76cm in circumference (the distance around the ball). Women players use a ball about 74cm in circumference. The rim of the hoop must be large enough to let the ball pass completely through. Basketballs for children come in a range of sizes and weights. A coach will be able to choose the best size for your age and ability.

Learn the lingo

Special names are given to different types of basketball shots. If you dribble up to the hoop and drop the ball right into the basket, it's called a 'dunk shot'. If you shoot and miss the basket completely, it's an 'air ball'.

THE US HALL OF FAME

The US Basketball Hall of Fame, in Springfield, Massachusetts, USA, is filled with basketball legends, history and trivia. You can meet players and watch them perform on the centre court, or have your photo taken beside the NBA (National Basketball Association) trophy.

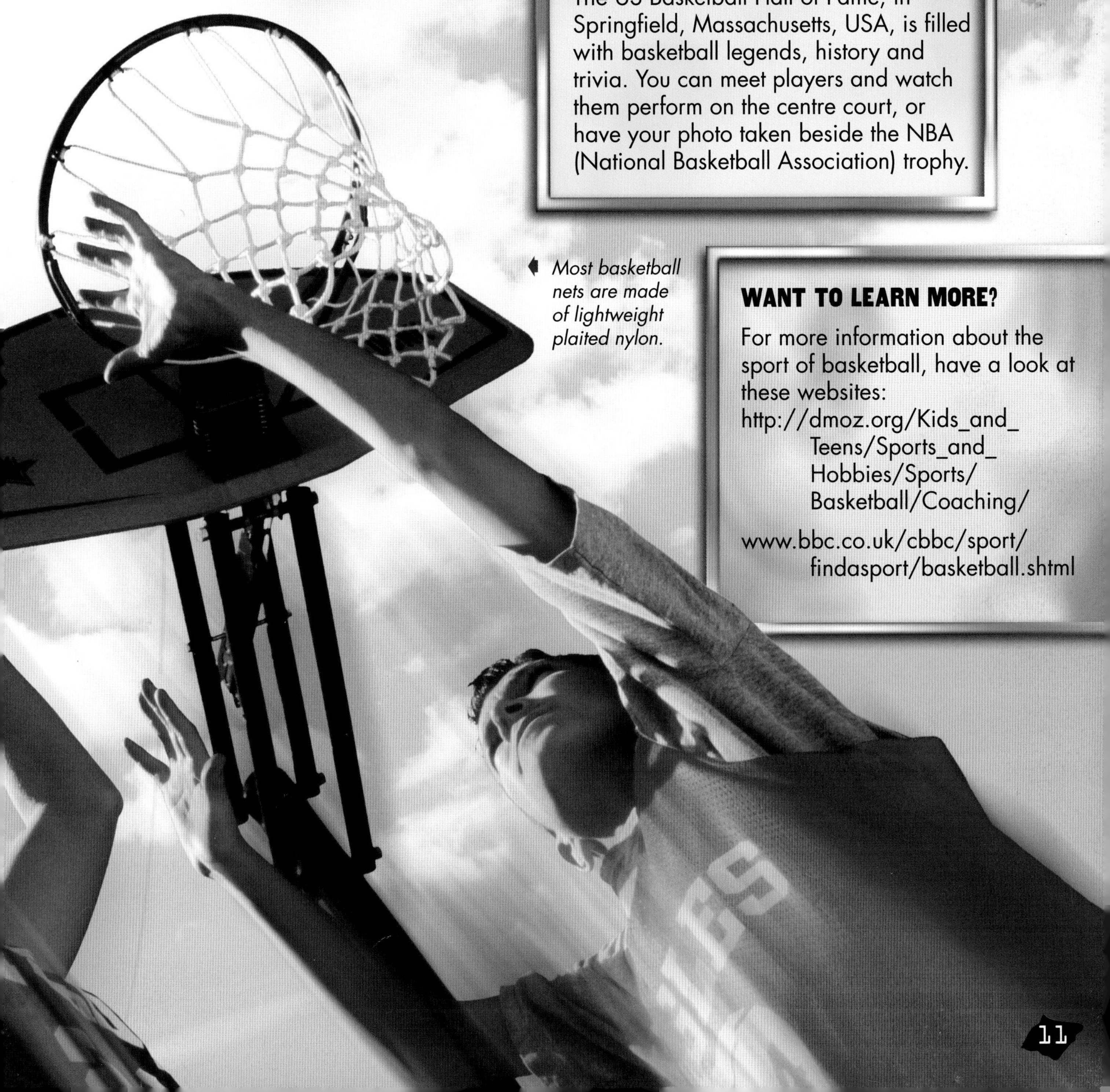

◀ *Most basketball nets are made of lightweight plaited nylon.*

WANT TO LEARN MORE?

For more information about the sport of basketball, have a look at these websites:

http://dmoz.org/Kids_and_
    Teens/Sports_and_
    Hobbies/Sports/
    Basketball/Coaching/

www.bbc.co.uk/cbbc/sport/
    findasport/basketball.shtml

NETBALL

NETBALL is a ball sport similar to basketball, but played mainly by women and girls. It is very popular in Australia, New Zealand, Jamaica, Great Britain, South Africa, Samoa, Barbados, Fiji and Trinidad.

Take your positions!

Netball is played on a court with a goalpost at either end. Two teams of seven players play against each other, but each player is only allowed in certain areas of the court, or they are considered **offside**. The players wear bibs with letters on that indicate one of seven positions: GS (goal shooter), GA (goal attack), WA (wing attack), C (centre), WD (wing defence), GD (goal defence) and GK (goal keeper). The aim of the game is to score as many goals as possible. Goals can only be scored by the GA and GS, from within an area of the court called the **goal circle**.

➡ *In netball, you cannot run with the ball, but you can turn on one foot to change direction before you throw.*

SILVER FERNS

At the 2006 Commonwealth Games in Melbourne, Australia, the New Zealand Silver Ferns took home the netball gold medal. The team takes its name from the silver fern, a tree species found only in New Zealand.

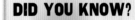

DID YOU KNOW?

Netball, like all other sports, has its own rules. The term 'playing the ball', for instance, means that once a player has caught the ball, he or she must either try to shoot a goal or pass it to another player within three seconds.

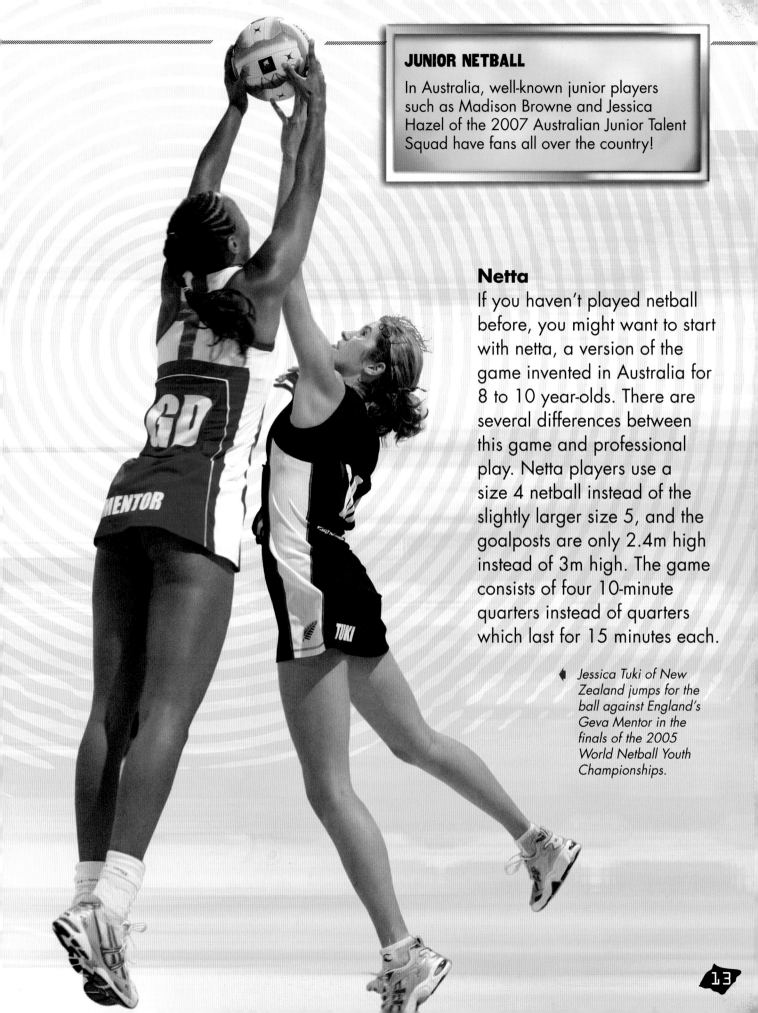

Netta

If you haven't played netball before, you might want to start with netta, a version of the game invented in Australia for 8 to 10 year-olds. There are several differences between this game and professional play. Netta players use a size 4 netball instead of the slightly larger size 5, and the goalposts are only 2.4m high instead of 3m high. The game consists of four 10-minute quarters instead of quarters which last for 15 minutes each.

Jessica Tuki of New Zealand jumps for the ball against England's Geva Mentor in the finals of the 2005 World Netball Youth Championships.

FOOTBALL is the most popular sport in the world. You may start by having a simple kick-around in the park with some friends, but before long you'll be wanting to play in the World Cup! In an organized game, football involves two teams of 11 players. The aim is to score more goals than the opposing team in 90 minutes.

The team

The players each have a position to play on the pitch. Defensive players tend to stay nearer their own goal to support the goalkeeper. **Midfielders** do much of the **tackling** – they try to take possession of the ball from the opposing team and pass it to the **strikers**. The strikers have the fun of trying to score goals! The goalkeeper's job is to stop any balls from getting into the net.

DAVID BECKHAM

David Beckham, former England captain, may be the world's most famous football player, but it's not just because he plays so well! He is also a hugely popular celebrity, appearing in all kinds of different magazines and on TV chat shows.

The referee

The referee's job is to make sure the players keep to the rules. If a player breaks the rules and **fouls**, the referee blows a whistle, stops the game and awards a **penalty** if necessary. The referee has two assistants who run up and down the **sidelines** and help him judge the game.

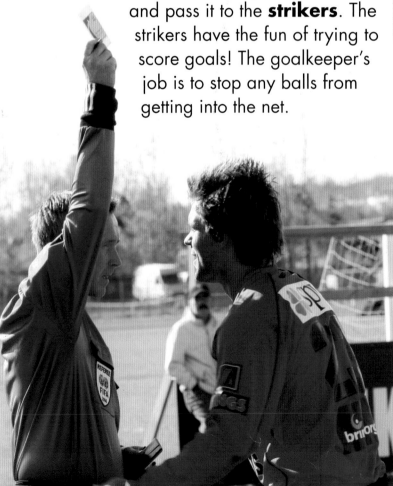

If the referee holds up a yellow card, it warns a player that he or she has committed a foul. If the player commits a second foul, he is given a red card and sent off the pitch.

SHIN PADS AND STUDS

Footballers wear shin pads under their long socks to protect the fronts of their legs (below the knees) from kicks. They also wear special boots with studs on the bottom to give them better grip on slippery or muddy fields.

Fighting fit

Football involves a lot of running, so practice sessions are designed to build up your strength. You might warm up before a game with a quick jog. To practise quick moves, try running and kicking a ball around a course of cones.

HEAD UP!

Professional footballers sometimes let the ball bounce off their heads in a move called a 'header'. Although it looks easy, it requires practice to hit the right area of the head and to get the ball to go in the right direction.

▶ *Women's football is popular all over the world, and every four years professional women footballers compete in the **FIFA** women's World Cup.*

Only the best

Football fans all over the world are keen supporters of the FIFA World Cup. In this famous competition, held every four years, national football teams from around the world compete to win the famous gold trophy. Fans in their millions watch the **qualifying matches** on TV. The live games are played outdoors under bright lights in front of thousands of spectators. The first men's World Cup was held in 1930, and the first women's World Cup in 1991.

The famous trophy

From 1930 to 1970, the winners were presented with the Jules Rimet trophy – named after the ex-FIFA president. In 1970, Brazil got to keep this cup after winning for the third time. It was replaced in 1974 by the FIFA World Cup.

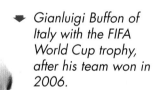

➤ *Gianluigi Buffon of Italy with the FIFA World Cup trophy, after his team won in 2006.*

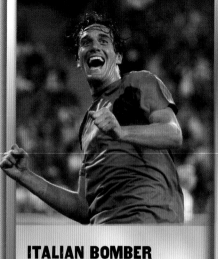

ITALIAN BOMBER

Luca Toni, nicknamed 'bomber', is one of the most admired players on Italy's national team. Although he may look small if you are watching him on TV, Toni is actually 1.98m tall. He scored two goals in the 2006 World Cup quarter-finals against Ukraine.

PELE

Pele, whose full name is Edson Arantes do Nascimento, is considered by many to be the world's best ever football player. He started playing for the Brazilian national team at the age of 16, and during his 22-year playing career he scored 1281 goals.

World Cup fever

Since the first World Cup was held, millions of fans have lined up to cheer for their nation's team. Fans show their support in lots of creative ways: some paint their faces and bodies, dye their hair or wear clothing in the colours of their country's flag (for example, red and white for England or green and yellow for Brazil). Fans also sing songs to support their team, and wave their national flags.

WORLD CUP WHEREABOUTS

Italy beat France to win the 2006 men's World Cup, held in Germany. The 2010 men's World Cup venue is South Africa, and the 2014 men's World Cup venue is South America. (Brazil is a strong contender to be the host.)

Fans filled the Olympic Stadium in Berlin, Germany, to watch a World Cup game between Brazil and Croatia in 2006. The stadium was built in the 1930s and seats more than 75 000 people.

RUGBY is an exciting game with a rich history. It developed in the 1800s from a form of football that had been played at Rugby School in England since the 1600s. Rugby is now popular not just in the UK and Ireland, but also in France, New Zealand, Australia and South Africa, among others.

THE RIGHT GEAR

If you want to play rugby, you'll need a pair of rugby shorts, a rugby shirt, a gum shield and an oval-shaped rugby ball. You'll also need a pair of boots with studs for grip. Some players also wear padding and a head guard for extra protection against injury.

How to score

Depending on the age of the players, the game can be played with 7, 10, 12, 13 or 15 players on a side. The aim is to move the oval-shaped ball to the other end of the field by carrying, **passing** or kicking it. Once the ball is near the other team's **try line**, there are several ways to score points. A player can cross the try line and, while holding the ball in their hands, touch the ground with the ball to score a 'try'. Or he or she can **drop kick** the ball over the crossbar between the opposing team's goal posts. (To read about the scoring system, see page 20.)

KICKING A GOAL

There are several ways to score a goal in rugby. After a team has been awarded a 'try', one of the players on that team can try to get additional points by attempting to kick the ball over the crossbar of the other team's goal posts. If successful, this is called a **conversion**. A **penalty kick** also earns the team points.

STARTING YOUNG

You can start playing Mini-rugby at the age of six, in the Under-7s level. Mini-rugby continues until you are aged 12, after which you can play in the Junior section. Girls and boys can play together until they become juniors.

← Catching an oval-shaped rugby ball can feel a little strange if you are used to a round ball. It's best to catch it with fingers spread apart, hands facing the ball and elbows bent.

Rugby codes

There are two distinct 'codes' of rugby: Rugby Union and Rugby League. Rugby Union is normally played with 15 players in the team. In Rugby League there are 13 players on the team. In both codes, teams include extra **reserve** players.

Point scoring

The scoring system is also different in Rugby Union and Rugby League. In Rugby Union, a try scores 5 points, a conversion 2 points and a **drop goal** 3 points. In Rugby League, a try scores 4 points, a conversion 2 points and a drop goal 1 point.

Tackling

To get the ball from an opposition player, players are allowed to tackle, or knock each other to the ground. This is what gives the game its rough-and-tumble reputation. Children do not usually learn to tackle until they are in the under-9s age group. Before this they play **touch** or **tag rugby**.

THROWING THE BALL

In rugby, players are allowed to throw the ball to another player. However, they are not allowed to throw the ball forwards! It can only be thrown to a player who is behind the ball-carrier, or to the side of them. It can, however, be kicked or carried forwards.

Rugby World Cup

According to some estimates, only the football FIFA World Cup and the summer Olympics are more popular spectator sports than the Rugby World Cup! The first Rugby World Cup, played in 1987, was hosted by Australia and New Zealand; the 2007 Rugby World Cup's venue is France; and the 2011 venue is New Zealand. It is held every four years.

◀ In rugby, you are allowed to run forwards holding the ball. You'll need to be very agile, because the opposition will try to get the ball from you.

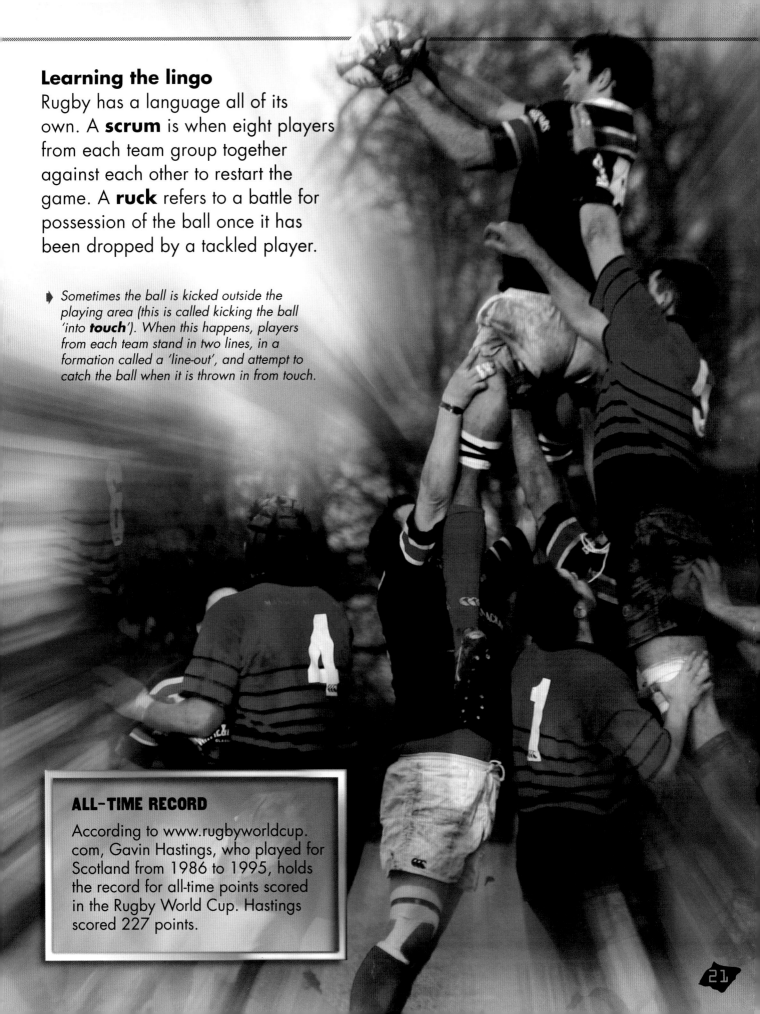

Learning the lingo

Rugby has a language all of its own. A **scrum** is when eight players from each team group together against each other to restart the game. A **ruck** refers to a battle for possession of the ball once it has been dropped by a tackled player.

▶ *Sometimes the ball is kicked outside the playing area (this is called kicking the ball 'into **touch**'). When this happens, players from each team stand in two lines, in a formation called a 'line-out', and attempt to catch the ball when it is thrown in from touch.*

ALL-TIME RECORD

According to www.rugbyworldcup.com, Gavin Hastings, who played for Scotland from 1986 to 1995, holds the record for all-time points scored in the Rugby World Cup. Hastings scored 227 points.

HANDBALL

HANDBALL is a team sport usually played in sports halls between teams of seven players. It is played at the Olympics. In the USA, another game called handball is also played, but it is more similar to squash than to team handball.

WORLD CHAMPIONS

The men's and women's handball world championships are organized by the International Handball Federation (IHF). In 2005, the Russian women's team (above) beat the Romanians. The IHF also organizes world championships for juniors, youth and beach handball. Be sure to check out www.ihf.info.

Team handball

The team sport of handball (also called European handball in the USA) is a fast, energetic sport in which the players may pass or dribble the ball in any direction. Players try to score in a football-like goal by throwing the ball from anywhere outside a 6-m semicircle.

➡ *An outdoor American handball court has three walls. Indoor courts usually have four walls.*

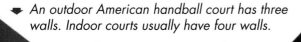

American handball

American handball is played on a walled court. In a 'singles' game, two players play against each other. In 'doubles', there are two teams of two players. There is also a practice version for three players. In singles, one player serves for points, dropping the ball to the floor and hitting it against the front wall. The other player receives the ball. A game is won by the first player or team to score 21 points, and a match goes to the first player or team to win two out of three games.

FUN FOR ALL AGES

Handball players as young as seven or eight years old, and as old as 90 play in tournaments.

A LONG HISTORY

Although the game has changed a lot since ancient times, most historians agree that the Greeks and Romans played a version of handball. The game also has a strong tradition in Ireland, where a version called **Gaelic handball** is played.

▶ In the team sport of handball, a player may hold the ball for only three seconds, and may take only three steps with the ball.

AMERICAN FOOTBALL

AMERICAN football is a popular spectator sport throughout the world, but nowhere is it more closely followed than in the USA, where thousands of people enjoy watching high school, college and professional games. It has its origins in the game of rugby, but it is different from rugby in many ways.

Simple objective

The goal in American football is simple: two teams of 11 players try to move the ball down the field and score points. Points are scored in a variety of ways: a 'touchdown', for instance, is worth 6 points. A touchdown is when the player moves the ball across the goal line, either by running with it or catching it from the **quarterback**. After a touchdown, the scoring team can get one extra point by kicking the ball through the goal posts.

TACKLING

American football involves tackling – trying to knock other players down in order to stop them from moving down the field with the ball. For protection, all players wear a helmet and pads all over their bodies. The quarterback needs a helmet that won't restrict his view, because he has to spot who to throw the ball to, or which **runner** to hand it to.

Touch American football

Touch or flag American football is a children's version of the game. Instead of tackling each other as they move the ball down the field, players just touch each other or pull a flag from their opponent's pocket.

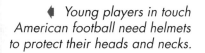

◀ *Young players in touch American football need helmets to protect their heads and necks.*

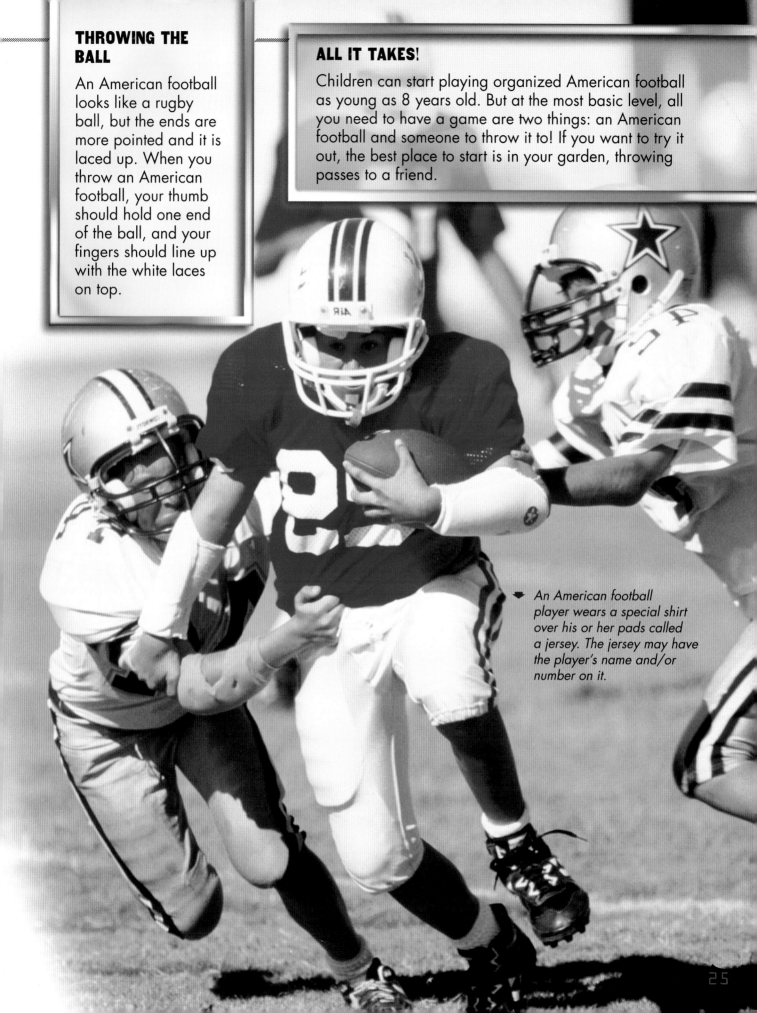

THROWING THE BALL

An American football looks like a rugby ball, but the ends are more pointed and it is laced up. When you throw an American football, your thumb should hold one end of the ball, and your fingers should line up with the white laces on top.

ALL IT TAKES!

Children can start playing organized American football as young as 8 years old. But at the most basic level, all you need to have a game are two things: an American football and someone to throw it to! If you want to try it out, the best place to start is in your garden, throwing passes to a friend.

An American football player wears a special shirt over his or her pads called a jersey. The jersey may have the player's name and/or number on it.

The major leagues

In the USA and Canada, American football teams play in two major leagues: the NFL (the National Football League) and the CFL (the Canadian Football League). Each league is made up of teams that play each other throughout the season. The NFL season ends with the Super Bowl. The best CFL teams play for the Grey Cup.

Super Bowl

The Super Bowl is the championship game played by the two top-ranking teams in the NFL. It is watched by at least 80 to 90 million viewers on TV in the USA alone, and is widely celebrated as a holiday.

↑ *The quarterback is often the leader of the team. He calls out coded signals to the other players to suggest what moves they should make.*

WORLD'S LOUDEST ROAR?

There are many records in professional American football, but one of the funniest involves the roar of a crowd at Mile High Stadium in Denver, Colorado. The fans there set a new world record for the loudest crowd: a reading of 128.74 decibels for 10 seconds. By comparison, the sound of a train horn about 1m away registers about 120 decibels.

Accurate kicking

In American football, the job of the team's kicker is to kick the ball as far downfield as possible, or to score by kicking the ball between the goal posts. Although this may look easy, kicking the ball accurately for 50m or more takes a lot of practice.

▶ *At the start of play, the centre player (opposite, in a black headband) 'hikes' the ball, meaning he or she passes it backwards between the legs, to the quarterback.*

Runners

Unlike in football, in which most players need to run a lot, the amount of running in American football depends on the position being played. The quarterback, for example, doesn't usually run with the ball very often, but a receiver, who runs down the field and tries to catch the ball that's being thrown by the quarterback, must be quick and agile.

POWDER PUFF AMERICAN FOOTBALL

Powder Puff American football is played in schools by girls, often as a charity fund-raising activity. It's a version of American flag football, in which the defensive team stop the ball-carrier not by tackling her, but by removing a flag from a belt around her waist.

27

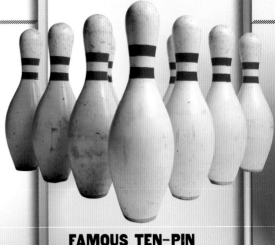

THERE ARE many different kinds of bowling games. One of the best-known is ten-pin bowling, played indoors in a bowling alley. Another is lawn bowls, played outdoors on a bowling **green**. Both versions involve rolling a ball along the ground towards a target some distance away.

Lawn bowls

Lawn bowls is played on a flat, grassy area called a green. The aim is to roll your balls along the ground to try and get them as close as you can to a small, white ball called the 'jack'. You'll need to knock your opponents' balls out of the way with your balls in order to get close to the jack.

FAMOUS TEN-PIN BOWLER

Tomas Leandersson of Sweden is one of the best ten-pin bowlers in the world. He has captained the European ten-pin bowling team, which plays a team from the USA every October for the Weber Cup.

Skittles

A very old version of bowling is skittles, which is said to date from the 14th century. It is played both indoors and outdoors. Indoor skittles is played in a skittle alley (from 6.4m to 9m long). The game involves trying to knock over nine pins using a wooden ball. Outdoor skittles, using a light, rubber ball, is a great game for children.

Bowls travel in a slightly curved path, because of the way they are shaped. If a player wants the ball to go to the left, he or she might need to aim slightly to the right.

Ten-pin and candlepin bowling

Ten-pin bowling involves rolling a 6.8kg bowling ball along a long, narrow lane towards a set of 10 pins, with the aim of knocking over as many of them as possible. Candlepin bowling, which is played in parts of the USA and Canada, uses a smaller ball (about 1kg), making it well suited for children's smaller hands. You usually get at least two tries at knocking down the pins.

Alley way

A bowling alley, where ten-pin bowling is played, is divided into many separate lanes so lots of people can play at once. After you roll your ball down the lane, a machine returns it to you down a separate narrow channel. The fallen or remaining pins are automatically cleared away, and a new set of pins is set up for the next player.

➤ *Players in a bowling alley often wear special bowling shoes, which have soles that don't mark the surface of the lane.*

amateur A person who plays a sport for pleasure, rather than being paid to do so.

attack, attacking The players who play in a forward position near the opponents' goal and attempt to score goals.

bump (volleyball) To hit the ball to another player on your team, using both forearms held close together.

coach An instructor who works with players to improve their skills.

conversion (rugby) A successful kick at the goalposts after a try has been awarded. In Rugby Union it scores 2 points.

defence, defending The defensive team, or the players who stay near their own goal and defend it when the other team attempts to score.

deflect To block or hit the ball so that it changes direction.

dig (volleyball) A pass made from close to the floor after receiving a spike. You hit the ball to a teammate, using the inside of the forearms.

drop goal (rugby) A goal scored by dropping the ball and kicking it over the crossbar of the goalposts. In Rugby Union it scores 3 points.

drop kick (rugby) A rugby move in which the player drops the ball and kicks it just as it touches the ground.

FIFA The letters stand for the Fédération Internationale de Football Association, French for the International Federation of Association Football.

foul To make an illegal move or to break a rule of the game.

Gaelic handball A sport in which players wear gloves and use their hands to hit a ball off the walls of an indoor court.

gain possession To get control of the ball from the other team.

goal circle (netball) A semicircle about 5m in front of the goalposts.

green The large, level area of short grass on which lawn bowls is played.

jump shot (basketball) To shoot a ball while jumping in mid air.

key (basketball) The area in front of the net, from which players can shoot the ball.

league A group of sports teams who compete among themselves.

midfielder (football) A player who mostly plays in the central area of the pitch.

offside When a player moves into an area of the court or pitch where he or she is not permitted, and a free pass or kick is awarded to the other team.

passing (rugby) To toss or throw the ball backwards to another player.

penalty A warning or punishment for breaking a rule. In football, a yellow card is a warning and a red card results in a player being sent off for the rest of the game and being banned from one or more following games.

penalty kick When a player breaks a rule, the other team is awarded a penalty kick at the goal to try to score.

professional A person who earns money by playing a sport.

qualifying matches Games played in the two years before the World Cup, to decide which teams will take part.

quarterback The leader of a team in American football. He or she suggests what tactics the players should use.

reserves Extra players on a team who may be called on to play if another player is injured, tired or not playing well.

ruck (rugby) A battle for possession of the ball once it has been dropped by a tackled player.

runners (American football) Players who run with the ball. For example, a receiver's job is to get into the open so he can catch a forward pass from the quarterback and then run with the ball; or the two running backs, who are handed the ball by the quarterback and then run with it.

scrum (rugby) A type of play used to restart the action. The forwards on both teams interlock arms to form a tunnel into which the ball is tossed.

serving (volleyball) To start the play for a new point by hitting the ball over the net.

set (volleyball) To hit the ball up into the air using both hands, often done so a teammate can slam it over the net.

sidelines The lines on a field or pitch that mark the edges of the playing area.

striker (football) An attacking player who tries to kick the ball into the goal.

tackling A way of gaining possession of the ball by taking it away from another player.

touch (rugby) The ball is said to be 'in touch' if it crosses the touch-line (sideline).

touch or **tag rugby** A game played by the under-9s or below, in which a player touches another player or removes a tag from his or her belt to force the player to pass the ball.

try line A goal line on a rugby field.

WEBSITES
Basketball
http://dmoz.org/Kids_and_Teens/Sports_and
    _Hobbies/Sports/Basketball/Coaching/
www.bbc.co.uk/cbbc/sport/findasport/
    basketball.shtml
Handball
www.ihf.info
Rugby
www.rugbyworldcup.com

Index